Making Peace with the Land of Australia

based on Principles for Promoting Peace with Planet Earth

Norman Habel

Making Peace with the Land of Australia

based on
Principles for Promoting Peace with Planet Earth

2019 Charles Strong Trust Lecture
by
Norman Habel

ATF Theology
Adelaide
2019

A Forum for Theology in the World
Volume 6, Issue 1, 2019

A Forum for Theology in the World is an academic refereed journal aimed at engaging with issues in the contemporary world, a world which is pluralist and ecumenical in nature. The journal reflects this pluralism and ecumenism. Each edition is theme specific and has its own editor responsible for the production. The journal aims to elicit and encourage dialogue on topics and issues in contemporary society and within a variety of religious traditions. The Editor in Chief welcomes submissions of manuscripts, collections of articles, for review from individuals or institutions, which may be from seminars or conferences or written specifically for the journal. An internal peer review is expected before submitting the manuscript. It is the expectation of the publisher that, once a manuscript has been accepted for publication, it will be submitted according to the house style to be found at the back of this volume. All submissions to the Editor in Chief are to be sent to: hdregan@atf.org.au.

Each edition is available as a journal subscription, or as a book in print, pdf or epub, through the ATF Press web site — www.atfpress.com. Journal subscriptions are also available through EBSCO and other library suppliers.

Editor in Chief
Hilary Regan, ATF Press

A Forum for Theology in the World is published by ATF Theology and imprint of
ATF (Australia) Ltd (ABN 90 116 359 963) and
is published twice or three times a year.

ISBN: 978-1-925612-96-7 soft
978-1-925612-97-4 hard
978-1-925612-98-1 epub
978-1-925612-99-8 pdf

ATF Press
PO Box 504
Hindmarsh SA 5007
Australia
www.atfpress.com

A Forum for Theology in the World Vol 6 No 1/2019

Table of Contents

Preface

This heart of this volume is based on a lecture I gave in honour of Charles Strong, my mentor in the pursuit of peace. On Armistice Day 2018, we held an Armistice Day Convocation to honour Charles Strong as a pioneer pacifist in Australia and collected our reflections in a volume entitled, *Remembering Pioneer Pacifist Charles Strong* (Habel 2018).

Some key lines from his famous *Thoughts on Armistice Day* capture the essence of his faith:

> *Jesus said, 'Love your enemies; do good to them that hate you; pray for them that persecute you'. I do not find in the celebration of Armistice Day any sign of this spirit, any prayer for Germans, Austrians, Serbians, Turks or Russians. Do they not need our prayers? Are they not our brothers? Are we not supposed, if one be overtaken in a fault, to 'restore such a one,' and so to 'bear one another's burdens?* (Habel 2018, 9).

Strong was an ardent advocate of peace at all levels of society and in international relations. He opposed the Boer War and the First World War, campaigning against conscription and refusing to sing the national anthem in church. For Strong, who was forced to leave the Presbyterian Church because of his stance on the doctrine of Atonement, God was not some omnipotent ruler on high but that almighty power called Love that permeates the cosmos and should govern all relationships in a society at peace.

In my Strong Trust Lecture in December 2019 I sought to extend the thinking of Strong to meet the current environmental crisis that requires a re-thinking of our relationship with nature and promoting peace with Planet Earth. I am extending the pacifism of Strong from 'peace on Earth' to 'peace with Planet Earth', a perspective that I am sure he would endorse.

I appreciate the editorial comments of Joh Wurst and Robert Crotty, a fellow member of the Charles Strong Trust.

A Forum for Theology in the World Vol 6 No 1/2019

Introduction

The impetus for this statement on *Making Peace with the Land of Australia*, explored in this volume, was a workshop at the Earth@ Peace conference in Melbourne in April 2019.

In each chapter, I will analyse one of the principles of the statement, outlining the basis of the principle and providing guidelines for actions to promote peace with Planet Earth, specifically here in the land of Australia.

The outline for each chapter will also include:

- the voice of Science
- the voice of the Christian Scriptures
- the voice of the Aboriginal custodians of Australia
- and the voice of Planet Earth

During the workshop at the Earth@Peace conference, a number of participants expressed a concern that we need to develop a more intimate and personal relationship with Planet Earth. Planet Earth, including our own land of Australia, has traditionally, in Western societies, been viewed as a material domain; humans do not have personal or spiritual relationships with Planet Earth. The very concept of 'peace with Planet Earth' challenges this tradition and invites us to reconsider how we relate to Planet Earth, the very source of our being. To help us explore this relationship I have included a brief section in each chapter which retrieves the voice of Planet Earth.

Also included are brief reflections from my life as a Planet Earth being, reflections that are designed to stimulate further reflection on how to facilitate the task of creating peace with Planet Earth in the land of Australia. In an Appendix, I include a version of the Vision of Charles Strong that I believe he would endorse were he alive today.

A Forum for Theology in the World Vol 6 No 1/2019

Making Peace with the Land of Australia based on the Principles for Promoting Peace with Planet Earth

---

As Planet Earth beings in Australia, we make the following statement as a step toward creating peace with Planet Earth, also known as Mother Earth, and especially with the land of Australia.

Principle 1: The Land of Australia Is the Mother of Planet Earth Beings Living in this Land

We confirm our identity as Planet Earth beings who live in the land of Australia, the mother who has nurtured us and now calls us to make peace with her.

Principle 2: Australia Is a Land Sustained in a Cosmic Sanctuary Called Planet Earth

We declare our intention to gain a deeper appreciation of how the land of Australia is embraced by a living planet called Planet Earth who also functions as a cosmic sanctuary that protects the land of Australia.

Principle 3: The Land of Australia Is an Eco-Wonder of Planet Earth

We need to discern afresh the deep web of ecological impulses that animate Planet Earth and learn to cooperate with them to create a harmonious community, a sacred biome in the land of Australia.

Principle 4: The Land of Australia Is a Wounded Child of Mother Earth

We regret the numerous acts of violence that the land of Australia has experienced at the hands of European settlers and we seek means of regeneration and restoration of the land previously preserved by her Aboriginal custodians.

Principle 5: Australia Is a Land with a Voice

We ask that the voices of the land of Australia and of her Aboriginal custodians be heard so that the government of this land becomes acutely aware not only of the environmental crisis but also of the inalienable rights of the land of Australia and her original custodians.

Principle 6: The Land of Australia Has a Sacred Site at Its Centre

The land of Australia is connected by many sacred sites; Uluru is an especially significant sacred site. Uluru could be viewed as a common spiritual symbol of peace for all Australians, regardless of their faith or orientation. All Australians could use Uluru as a spiritual symbol to express peace between themselves and Planet Earth.

Chapter One
Principle 1: The Land of Australia Is the Mother of Planet Earth Beings

We confirm our identity as Planet Earth beings who live in the land of Australia, the mother who has nurtured us and now calls us to make peace with her.

Principle 1 identifies the land of Australia as our mother and the human beings living in the Land of Australia as Planet Earth beings. This identification that is vital if we are to move beyond the traditional mindset that identifies human beings as superior to all other living beings on Planet Earth.

It is time to acknowledge

- Planet Earth as the source of our being
- the land of Australia as our chosen home
- Planet Earth being as our true identity.

The Challenge

This principle challenges us relate to Planet Earth

- as the source of our existence rather than a source of wealth
- as a living mother rather than lifeless matter
- as the source of our identity as Planet Earth beings.

This principle also challenges us to relate to the Land of Australia:

- as a land that is to be cherished as our home
- as a parent who has nurtured humans for millennia
- as a mother who urges us to make peace with her.

The Voice of Science

The voice of science, in spite of dismissed popular traditions about 'Mother Earth' in the Western world, reminds us that Planet Earth is indeed our mother and that we are Planet Earth beings. As children of our mother, Planet Earth, we recognise how Planet Earth has nurtured us for millennia. Our daily existence is dependent, for example, on the magnetic forces of Planet Earth. Macy reminds us that matter

> *is made of rock and soil. It too is pulled by the magma that circulates through our planet heart and roots such molecules into biology. Earth pours through us, replacing each cell in the body every 7 years...we ingest and excrete Earth. We are made from Earth. I am that. You are that!* (Macy 1996, 501).

According to scientists, Planet Earth was formed 4.6 billion years ago. It was then inhospitable; there were no living organisms. One billion years later numerous embryonic life forms, our ancestors, inhabited Planet Earth. Planet Earth had become a cosmic womb, a unique abode for life to be born and flourish.

Billions of years after the 'big bang' came the 'tiny touch' when the first chemicals and elements needed for life came together to create organic life, the first-born life forms of Planet Earth: the primordial Planet Earth beings.

David Suzuki reminds us that all the descendants of Planet Earth, are all our relatives, and constitute a remarkable family on whom we ultimately depend for life; our survival on Planet Earth is possible because of our primordial ancestors.

> *Earth's family, though, is truly amazing. Great horned owls, African elephants, domestic cats, chestnut trees, killer whales, lady bugs, McIntosh apples—our relatives come in an incredible number of forms. There's a word for that tremendous variety—biodiversity. Bio means life, a diversity means difference... This abundance of species is not an accident or waste. Like air, water, soil and energy from the sun, it seems that biodiversity is necessary for life* (Suzuki & Vanderlinden 1999, 68).

Evolution may now be a basic subject in the school science curriculum or in public discussion. It is important, however, not to separate this subject as a field that is 'mere' science. This subject, along with zoology, biology and botany, deals with the experience of our mother, Planet Earth, and our kin: all the Planet Earth living beings on this planet. Evolution is part of our family history and our life story as Planet Earth beings here in the Land of Australia.

Image of a primordial womb.

Planet Earth, however, is not only the source of our existence, but also our habitat in the cosmos. More specifically, our habitat is a unique domain on Planet Earth, and our chosen home: the land of Australia.

The time has come to learn from Mother Earth about how to make peace with Planet Earth by living at peace with the land of Australia.

We also need the generate opportunities to explore how our biodiverse ancestors have been dependent on the care given them by Planet Earth over the millennia. Our diverse predecessors have all been dependent on Planet Earth for their breath, their food, their habitat in different ways in different periods of history. The genes and the DNA that human children have inherited have been developed over the years in generations of children born of Planet Earth and, more recently, those born of the land of Australia.

The Voice of the Christian Scriptures

Our identity as Planet Earth beings is also acknowledged in the Bible, even though this truth is rarely acknowledged. The following precise translation of Genesis 2:4b–7 demonstrates that identity.

> *In the day that the Lord God made the earth (*ʾeretz*) and the skies, when no plant of the field was yet in the earth (*ʾeretz*) and no herb of the field had yet sprung up—for the Lord God had not caused it to rain upon the ground (*ʾadamah*), and there was no Earth Creature to till the ground (*ʾadamah*); but a stream (*ʿed*) would rise from the earth (*ʾeretz*), and water the whole face of the ground (*ʾadamah*)—then the Lord God formed the Earth Creature (*ʾadam*) from the Dirt (*ʾaphar*) of the ground (*ʾadamah*), and breathed into its nostrils the breath of life; and the Earth Creature became a living being (*nephesh*).*

The story of the origin of human beings in Genesis 2 makes it clear that the Dirt (*ʾaphar*) of which *ʾadam*, the first Earth Creature is composed, is taken from the matter we would recognise today as Planet Earth. According to the Bible, we are the descendants of the first Earth Creature, the first Earth being.

A key biblical text, often ignored however, is Psalm 139:13–15:

> *Thou didst form my inward parts,*
> *Thou didst knit me together in my mother's womb.*
> *I praise Thee, for Thou art fearful and wonderful.*
> *Wonderful are Thy works!*
> *Thou knowest me right well;*

My frame was not hidden from Thee,
when I was made in secret,
intricately woven in the depths of Earth.

In the words of this psalmist, the depths of Planet Earth are the womb in which humans are formed in secret by the mysterious mind of the Creator. Planet Earth is indeed our mother and we are Planet Earth beings, born of Planet Earth matter; this is a principle we need to acknowledge publicly.

While there are several stories about the origin of Planet Earth in the Bible, the story of the birth of Planet Earth in Genesis 1 is evocative. On the third day, in the Genesis 1 creation story, God issues a new order. God does ***not*** say, 'Let there be Earth', because Earth already exists in the waters of the deep, the cosmic womb. Instead God says, 'Let the waters separate (= burst) and let Earth appear'. Planet Earth is not created out of nothing, but born out of the primal waters. Planet Earth is born when the cosmic womb waters break!

Furthermore, God does ***not*** say 'Let there be life'. God says 'Let Earth bring forth life'. On the third day the ground of Planet Earth brings forth all kinds of vegetation—the first forms of life in the Bible. On the fifth day, the waters of Planet Earth bring forth all kinds of living creatures, including birds, fish and sea monsters. On the same day, the ground of Planet Earth brings forth everything that walks and crawls on the ground. Planet Earth is a co-creator, the source of all living creatures in this creation story.

Throughout the Old Testament, we can meet our kin in whom the pulse of life is beating in a range of ways. The pulse of life in a squid is different from that in a squirrel and the pulse of life in a eucalyptus tree is different from the pulse of life in an elephant. Yet all our kin experience that same pulse of the Spirit that originated in the first forms of life on Planet Earth.

Psalm 104.27–30 speaks about the Spirit as the impulse that stirs the pulse of life in the ground, the soil of Planet Earth and sustains all creatures. Mother Earth is animated by the Spirit from her first birth; this Spirit animation pulses in every baby born of Planet Earth. Every form of life in the land of Australia experiences the pulse of life that emanates from Mother Earth, the Creator Spirit that animates Planet Earth.

In this volume, the designation 'Creator Spirit' refers to the spiritual life force that creates, permeates and animates Planet Earth. This life force is identified as the Rainbow Spirit by the Rainbow Spirit elders, as the Creator and the Spirit in the Old Testament Scriptures and as Christos or Logos in the Gospel of John and the Pauline Epistles.

The Voice of the Aboriginal Custodians of Australia

We can also learn from our Aboriginal elders that the land of Australia is the Mother of their people; they belong to country and are born of the ground of the land that they belong to and gives them their identity, their belonging. This is not like the Western concept of ownership as power over; they understand that they are custodians of this land. This is a reciprocal relationship with mutual benefits and responsibilities. The land of Australia is not only the source of their physical nature; it is also the source of their spiritual identity, their Dreaming. In his book, *The Land Our Mother*, Patrick Dodson clarifies the nuances of this relationship.

> *The land is a living place made up of sky, clouds, rivers, trees, the wind, the sand; and the Spirit has planted my spirit there, in my own country. It is something—and yet it is not a thing—it is a living entity. It belongs to me, I belong to it. I rest in it. I come from there* (1973, 53).

According to the Rainbow Spirit elders, the land is alive within; it is filled with the life-forces of all species on Earth. The ground itself is alive, dynamic and creative. In the words of the Rainbow Spirit elders, the

> *identity of Aboriginal Peoples is determined by their deep connection with the land . . . In each Aboriginal person there is land and spirit. Both of these link each one of us with the land and the Creator Spirit in the land. For us Aboriginal People to know our true identity, it is vital for us to know the specific place in the land to which we belong* (Rainbow Spirit Elders 2007, 38).

For Aboriginal people, 'our land' means 'my own country', as Patrick Dodson demonstrates (1973, 53).

We, like our Aboriginal brothers and sisters, also belong to the land of Australia; it is our Mother, our land, our home. Our mission, therefore is not only to acknowledge our identity as Planet Earth beings, but to serve and preserve our land in such a way as to create a peace that means living in harmony with all life within the land of Australia—everything from the ants to the atmosphere, from the frogs to the forest, from the lizards to the landscape.

The peace we are called to create has a rich precedent in the close relationship of the Aboriginal peoples with the land—the country—of each Aboriginal community—language group—in the land of Australia.

The Voice of Planet Earth

I am Planet Earth
the Mother Earth and custodian
of all living beings on Planet Earth
including everything within the land of Australia.
I invite you
to explore not only your origins
as Planet Earth beings
who know the pulse of life
that emanated from me
since the day of your evolution,
but also the deep bond that exists between us,
a bond we need to strengthen
to create peace into the future.

Planet Earth Peace Mission

When we appreciate that Planet Earth is our Mother Earth and that we are indeed Planet Earth beings, it is time to make our identity known publicly and not to hide our origins. Christians are not only children of God by faith or baptism; they are also children of Mother Earth. However, as a public event, this naming could be quite controversial. However, Psalm 139:15 declares unequivocally that this is our heritage: 'I was made in secret, intricately woven in the depths of Earth'.

> *Today we publicly recognise that Planet Earth is indeed our planet Mother and that we, her children, really care about her and promise to make peace with her. Today we are proud to identify ourselves as Planet Earth beings.*

A symbol that might be employed to emphasise this initiative is that of Planet Earth with a human foetus inside a global womb. This icon could be unveiled in a drama relating to Planet Earth about to give birth. Perhaps we could set aside a day of the year to be the birthday of all Planet Earth beings, human and other than human, and invite Mother Earth to celebrate with us.

Reflections

In response to the voice of Planet Earth here in the land of Australia I have, over the years, reflected personally about my identity as a Planet Earth being. I include one of these reflections to stimulate further discussion about ways of creating peace with Planet Earth.

Planet Earth's Pulse

Once I discovered Planet Earth was my true mother
and that I was a Planet Earth being,
I realised that Planet Earth is alive
pulsing
deep within her core
and across her crust;
a vibrating mass of living matter.
How do I feel the pulse of Planet Earth?
Put my finger on the throbbing extremities,
and connect with the life-forces,
the hidden impulses
of life
that permeate this planet?

If I hold a wild flower in my fingers,
place my hands on the trunk of a tree,
hold the beak of a pelican
or grasp a slippery silver eel,
will I feel the pulse of Planet Earth?

The impulses of Planet Earth to live,
to sing, to evoke wonder,
are in every throbbing cell of Planet Earth beings,
in every life-force in the land of Australia,
in every scene in the landscape.

Finally
when I feel the pulse of Planet Earth
with my hands in the air
my feet on the ground
feeling the throb of life
in every movement of Planet Earth,
I am at peace with my planet Mother.

Chapter Two
Principle 2: Australia Is a Land Sustained in a Cosmic Sanctuary Called Planet Earth

---

We declare our intention to gain a deeper appreciation of how the land of Australia is embraced by a living planet called Earth who also functions as a cosmic sanctuary that protects the land of Australia.

Principle 2 not only recognises the land of Australia as an amazing biome on Planet Earth that was formed billions of years ago and nourishes a world of living organisms. This biome is characterised by a unique beneficial relationship between plants, animals, climate and soil, providing a haven—a cosmic sanctuary where amazing forms of life flourish. It is time to thank Planet Earth for being a home where we are safe and the land of Australia for being a haven of hope for peace on Planet Earth.

The Challenge

This principle challenges us relate to Planet Earth:

- as a unique planet on which living organisms evolve
- as a cosmic sanctuary where these organisms are sustained and protected
- as a piece of stardust quivering with living mystery.

This principle also challenges us to relate to the land of Australia:

- as a biome of Planet Earth that we share with billions of living organisms
- as a unique safe space within a cosmic sanctuary
- as haven where we can celebrate the mysteries of life.

The Voice of Science

Planet Earth was once a blazing ball of gases spinning through space. On such a ball of fire no life was possible for billions of years. But now Planet Earth is a sanctuary, a safe place, a protected haven where living creatures flourish. Planet Earth is precious—a sacred space to preserve for posterity.

The principle that Planet Earth is a safe place, a biome where diverse life-forms flourish in the cosmos, is grounded in the investigations of space age scientists who use the Hubble telescope to view, and deep space probes of nearby planets to explore, why life can survive and flourish on Planet Earth and nowhere else in the cosmos.

Two reasons Planet Earth is a safe cosmic sanctuary are:

- the thin blue line on the surface of Planet Earth called the atmosphere
- the invisible dark force in the depths of Planet Earth called gravity.

Unlike other planets, the atmosphere of Planet Earth provides a protective blanket that wards off the harsh destructive forces of solar radiation, yet allows and retains sufficient warmth from the sun for life to flourish. This thin blue line is the shield that makes Planet Earth an amazing sanctuary in our solar system.

Planet Mercury has almost no atmosphere. Planet Venus has an atmosphere of sulphuric acid. The atmosphere of Planet Mars has been destroyed.

Moreover, the atmosphere of Planet Earth is oxygen-rich, maintaining the necessary mixture of gases and their continual movement for life to flourish—whether by breathing the air or swaying in the wind.

The other major factor that keeps Planet Earth safe is gravity, that force which holds the atmosphere close to Planet Earth's surface. Gravity projects an amazing magnetic force from the centre of Planet Earth that protects our Planet Earth from the fierce solar winds that bombard all planets. Gravity ensures Planet Earth is a cosmic sanctuary, a safe place in the solar system. And the land of Australia is a unique haven of hope within the cosmic sanctuary, one of the many diverse habitats of Planet Earth.

Evolution also reveals an exciting scientific story of the development and survival of life-forms on this cosmic sanctuary called Planet Earth, from genetic molecules to gigantic dinosaurs. The earliest tiny life-forms—our oldest ancestors—were born in the ocean. Some eventually made it onto the land and evolved into plants and then animals. Millions of species evolved over millions of years. A wild and wonderful family has survived: a diverse family we have learned to love in the land of Australia—a family of whales and wombats, kangaroos and koalas!

How many life forms evolved from these primal ancestors and survived is a mystery that scientists continue to explore. As we explore the need for peace with Planet Earth, we are reminded that billions of years ago, all life forms survived in a very different world. Planet Earth care was always part of the role of Planet Earth as the source of our existence.

The Voice of the Christian Scriptures

In the biblical tradition, Planet Earth is not only a sanctuary that protects life, but also a sanctuary for an underlying presence we call the Creator Spirit.

Life is more than a collection of living things. Life is a sacred force. Life is a presence that permeates our planet, a mystery that we are summoned not only to sustain but also to celebrate with all other living things (Ps 148).

The origins of life on our planet are amazing. Just as amazing is its deep-life dimension. Planet Earth has, deep within, a life-force that animates and stirs life, a life-force that we associate with the Spirit of the Creator (see Ps 104:29–30). Planet Earth is a living sanctuary filled with Life emanating from the Creator Spirit.

A fascinating insight from the Bible is that the Hebrew word for wind *(ruach)* is also the word for air, atmosphere, breath and spirit. The atmosphere we breathe is, according to the Scriptures, the very breath/spirit of the Creator Spirit. The breath of life that animated Adam, also animates all Planet Earth beings today—and the planet in which we live.

Planet Earth is also a sanctuary for the presence of the Creator Spirit, the source of life. The Presence of God (*kabod YHWH*), sometimes translated as 'the glory of God', appears on Mt Sinai as a stunning fire-cloud, a burning presence that Moses experiences for forty days. That same fire-cloud then 'fills' the tabernacle—and is a concentrated manifestation of God's presence in the temple in Jerusalem.

Later, however, when Isaiah is worshipping in the temple, he hears the famous chorus of the seraphim we associate with the *Sanctus.*

> *Holy, holy, holy is the Lord of hosts,*
> *the whole Earth is filled with his Presence.*

The message is clear! The whole Planet Earth is 'filled' with a living Presence. Planet Earth is therefore like the tabernacle and the temple of old: a sacred place to worship with the Creator Spirit. According to the Scriptures, Planet Earth is a shimmering living sanctuary in the cosmos, a sacred site like Uluru in the Aboriginal world of the land of Australia.

The Voice of the Aboriginal Custodians of Australia

The Aboriginal Peoples of the land of Australia have long recognised that nature of this land as sacred, as a living sanctuary. Chapter Three of *Rainbow Spirit Theology* (Rainbow Spirit Elders, 2007) describes in detail how the Rainbow Spirit elders understood the role of the Rainbow Spirit active in the land of Australia.

> *From the beginning, the Rainbow Spirit has been and still is present deep within the land.*
>
> *The Rainbow Spirit is the life-giving power of the Creator Spirit active in the world. The Creator Spirit filled the land with numerous life-forces and spiritual forces. The Creator Spirit causes these life-forces to emerge from the land.*
>
> *Human beings were also created from the land by the Creator Spirit and eventually return to the Spirit who is present in the land.*
>
> *Human beings are entrusted with the responsibility to co-operate with the Creator Spirit both to care for and to activate the life-forces within the land.*

These headings from Chapter Three of *Rainbow Spirit Theology* illustrate how these Aboriginal elders experienced the sacred nature of their land, a living sanctuary they were commissioned to activate and sustain. The early missionaries may well have described this worldview as blatant animism.

A sensitivity to the life-forces of Planet Earth as a cosmic sanctuary moves us today to acknowledge the extreme value of the faith and ethos of the Aboriginal custodians who functioned as 'priests' who preserved and sustained the land of Australia as sacred for millennia.

The Voice of Planet Earth

I am Planet Earth.
I am more than the source of your
existence and identity as Planet Earth beings.
I am also the reason why you
and all other life beings
on the land of Australia
continue to survive and flourish.
I am a sanctuary,
a sacred site in the cosmos
that protects you
and calls you to be custodians
at peace with me.

Planet Earth Peace Mission

If we are to make Peace with Planet Earth, the fate and welfare of all species in the land of Australia are also our concern. We need to ask: what has happened to our kin in this continent in the past? We need to explore what is happening to our brothers and sisters of the animal world amid the trauma of climate change—whether these relatives live on the Great Barrier Reef, at the South Pole or in the remains of an ancient Tasmanian forest.

Scientists have identified five periods over the past 500 million years when large numbers of our relatives have become extinct. Planet Earth's vitality is demonstrated as Planet Earth recovers its previous level of biodiversity following each extinction. We are now in a sixth extinction crisis—one created by human beings. We are now killing off species—our kin—faster than ever before in Planet Earth's history.

It is now part of our Planet Earth care commitment to make our planet, our cosmic sanctuary, safe for all the threatened species in our living family tree. Planet Earth care also means protection of all species and habitats in the haven of the land of Australia.

The task of a Planet Earth-conscious community is to develop a peace mission that recognises that Planet Earth is not just another puny planet in the ever-expanding universe, but an amazing cosmic sanctuary where we are given the unbelievable privilege of residing as living beings.

One plan of action for a peace mission is for community groups and organisations that are ready to recognise the nature of Planet Earth as a cosmic sanctuary, and the need to set aside a time to celebrate the wonders and mysteries of Planet Earth as a cosmic sanctuary. On this day, artists, thinkers and visionaries will unite to highlight the unique nature of the land of Australia, part of Planet Earth's cosmic living sanctuary exploding with life is all its amazing diverse forms and beauty.

Churches might link this day with *The Season of Creation,* a festival that originated in the land of Australia and is now celebrated by many churches around the world in September; (for details, see www.seasonofcreation.com.au).

Reflections

In response to the voice of Planet Earth here in the land of Australia I have, over the years, reflected personally about my identity as a Planet Earth being. I include one of these reflections to stimulate further reflection about ways of creating peace with Planet Earth.

A Microcosm

Once I realised I was a Planet Earth being
and that Earth was indeed my Planet Earth mother,
I began to explore
my new world,
my new cosmology.

It is one thing to realise I am made of clay
like other clay creatures,
and that I have evolved with a pulse of life
similar to that of a platypus.

But Planet Earth!
Planet Earth is a mass of mystery,
a panorama of wonders,
a cosmic sanctuary,
to be read as divine revelation
and a cosmic companion.

Planet Earth is an embryo,
a sacred microcosm
of the cosmos
where we can explore the mysteries
of the universe residing in Planet Earth
the cosmic sanctuary that protects us
in the land of Australia.

Chapter Three
Principle 3: The Land of Australia Is an Eco-Wonder of Planet Earth

We need to discern afresh the deep web of ecological impulses that animate Planet Earth and learn to cooperate with them to create a harmonious planet community, a sacred biome on the land of Australia.

Principle 3 recognises that the land of Australia is an ecological wonder on Planet Earth, an amazing web of interrelated forces, mysteries and mazes, a biome within which each of us is connected, and to which each of us belongs. The time has come to embrace ecology as an exciting journey through which we can discover our intimate connection with the impulses of the cosmos so we can create peace with Planet Earth.

The Challenge

This principle challenges us to find the amazing ecological interconnections that affect our relationship with Planet Earth, including

- the forces of gravity and the survival of the planet
- the worms in the ground and the food we eat
- the ocean currents and wild weather patterns.

This principle also challenges us to relate to the land of Australia:

- as a habitat, a biome of Planet Earth interlaced with ecological wonders
- as a land interconnected with all the forces of nature
- as a land where we can discern our close relationship with every living thing.

The Voice of Science

Planet Earth has been likened to a living organism. The numerous different life forms are dependent on each other in a mutually beneficial way. In other words, it can be said that Planet Earth is tantamount to

- a living community where biodiversity enhances health, happiness and peace
- a vibrant habitat where, through death, all materials are recycled for life!

The interconnection of all species is made clear in the words of David Suzuki, in a quote that is itself a valuable maze of mysteries worth exploring.

> No *species exists in isolation from all others. In fact, today's estimated 30 million species are all connected through the intersection of their life-cycles—plants depend on specific insect species to pollinate them, fish move through vast expanses of the ocean feeding and being fed upon by other species, and*

> *birds migrate halfway around the world to raise young on the brief explosion of insect populations in the Arctic. Together* ***all species make up one immense web of interconnections*** *that binds all beings to each other and the physical component* (Suzuki & McConnell 1997, 137–38).

When it was discovered that Planet Earth was round, the flat-Earth cosmology of humans changed radically.

Just as radical is to need to embrace ecology as basic to our very existence; we must again embrace a new cosmology, an understanding of the world as a maze of inter-connected mysteries—both physical and spiritual.

Today we are confronted by the mystery of how every force in the cosmos is somehow connected, whether through light-years of time, across wide worlds of space or dark masses of matter. In our home web, the forces of gravity, motion and anti-gravity bind us together in a tiny planet where life is possible. Amid the wide web of cosmic ecosystems, our home in the land of Australia is an amazing local eco-wonder amidst a universe of eco-mysteries.

Planet Earth is not a lifeless ball of stardust; it is a vibrant community of forces and presences that interact and communicate with each other to enable life. All Planet Earth's components—from the mountains to the forests, from the seas to the ice caps—are part of a complex living entity, a biome called Planet Earth.

In other words, the wondrous web of inter-related forces called Planet Earth is a web of living wonders, a community of communicating forces, a maze of endlessly moving mysteries. In the land of Australia we live in a wondrous eco-web of close relationships, both local and cosmic, from the sand hills of the Red Desert to the flow of the mighty Murray.

The Voice of the Christian Scriptures

In the past we have tended to read the Bible from a dualistic perspective in which the components of the cosmos were separate entities. Heaven was separate from Earth. The sun was separate from Planet Earth. Humans were separate from other creatures. The sea was separate from the land. Ecology challenges us to discover how everything is connected and related. Is this challenge found anywhere in the Bible?

According to the Book of Job, God takes Job on a tour of the cosmos—a tour that might well be designated an eco-tour (Job 38–40). Job is challenged, at the outset, to grasp the 'design' of the cosmos—to discern how the components of the cosmos belong together in one grand blueprint.

Job is confronted, not only with a mass of wondrous habitats in creation, but also with the mystery of where they belong in the cosmos and how they are interrelated in a biome: a web of living beings. Job's experience on that journey is tantamount to what today we would call an 'ecological conversion' (see Job 38–39).

Job is also confronted by the mysteries of astronomy, the architecture of Earth, the relationship of the ocean to the land and the innate Wisdom that guides the forces of the weather.

The ecological dimension of God's design is especially evident when God challenges Job to grasp how the laws of space are related to, and involved in, establishing order or peace on Planet Earth (Job 38:31–33). What is the connection between forces in space and the design of Earth? This is an ecological challenge that astronomers still face. In these verses, we sense how the wise of the ancient Near East explored the interrelationship of external forces such as gravity and their influence on Earth (see Habel 2015, chapter 3).

The Voice of the Aboriginal Custodians of Australia

The spirituality of Aboriginal Peoples in the land of Australia may well be called eco-spirituality, as Eddie Kneebone observes,

> *Aboriginal spirituality is the belief and the feeling within yourself that allows you to become part of the whole environment—not the built environment, but the natural environment...Birth, life and death are all part of it and you welcome each. Aboriginal spirituality is the belief that all objects are living and share the same soul or spirit that Aboriginals share. Therefore, all Aboriginals have a kinship with the environment. The soul or spirit is common—only the shape of it is different, but no less important* (Mudrooroo 1995, 33–34).

For Australia's Aboriginal Peoples, land is the eco-force that unites all biomes and spheres of the land of Australia, whether they be—in Western language—animate or inanimate, material or spiritual, geological or cultural. And Michael Dodson makes this relationship abundantly clear.

> *To understand our law, our culture and our relationship with the physical and spiritual world, you must begin with the land. Everything about Aboriginal society is inextricably interwoven with, and connected to, the land. Culture is the land, the land and spirituality of Aboriginal people, our cultural beliefs or reason for existence is the land. You take that away and you take away our reason for existence. We have grown the land up. We are dancing, singing and painting for the land. We are celebrating the land. Removed from our lands, we are literally removed from ourselves* (1997, 41).

Land is a pivotal habitat, a biome where the integrating forces of the ecosystems of the land of Australia are discerned and experienced by the Aboriginal Peoples of this land. Their nuanced ecological consciousness may serve as a model to help us discern how the ecosystems relate to our land and how we can best live at peace with these systems.

The Voice of Planet Earth

I am Planet Earth.
I am a vibrant community,
a wondrous web of life-forces
and dynamic cosmic forces
that interrelate throughout my body
in such a way as to effect
harmony and peace
when free
from unwarranted interruption.

Planet Earth Peace Mission

An eco-peace mission requires that we move beyond viewing our Planet Earth and our home in the land of Australia as consisting of a series of discrete habitats that may be viewed in isolation and analysed separately. We need to create an everyday awareness that each of us is connected to a fascinating web of mysteries, a web of biomes linking the eco-systems of the planet, animals and plants and all living things, and our local landscapes.

One helpful activity involves inviting members of the local community—whether church, town or neighbourhood—to take an eco-tour of the location in which we live. Through this tour, we can explore how all living things, communities and natural phenomena are interconnected. There may be only a few degrees of separation between humans, but there will also be close connection in terms of features of the location—landscape, roads, homes, trees, gardens, compost bins, people, pets, birds, insects, reptiles . . .

A part of this project could be determining the ecological footprint of the community and its various members. These connections may form an eco-map of a given location to will help people realise how they are connected not only with fellow Planet Earth beings on the land of Australia but also with the wind, the atmosphere, the soil, gravity and other interrelated forces in our habitat: the places we live.

Telling stories of past connections between people and nature may also help us to remember just how vital our past bonds with nature have been—and help us to encourage new positive relationships with all life forces and forms on Planet Earth.

Another course of action is to explore the many ways in which the forces, laws, biomes and habitats and realities of nature are interconnected. For example, how is my breath connected with the ocean? How is my body connected with the worms in the soil? How is my brain connected with gravity? And how have I interrupted interrelationships between these forces of nature?

Reflections

In response to the voice of Planet Earth here in the land of Australia I have, over the years, reflected personally about my identity as a Planet Earth being in this eco-wonder called Earth. I include one of these reflections to stimulate further reflection about ways of creating peace with Planet Earth.

Ecology

Then came the big surprise,
like a last minute revelation
to a tired old prophet
waiting in the wings of Wisdom.

The big word was ecology.
I had always considered ecology
but another science,
complementing biology, physics and psychology.

No!
Ecology, I discovered, is a new worldview,
a challenging cosmology that would make Galileo cringe;
a consciousness revolution!

Some compare ecology with a web
where everything is connected
but without any sacred spider on the scene.
Some speak of a whirlpool
of animate and inanimate forces
bouncing and balancing in the wind of time.

Ecology means
everything is related socially, biologically
and spiritually!

And Planet Earth?
Planet Earth is a wondrous womb
in which all the land forces and life forces
activated by innate Wisdom
combine to create new lives,
mysteries and peace in Terra Australis,
a land protected in a cosmic sanctuary
called Planet Earth, my planet mother!

Chapter Four
Principle 4: The Land of Australia Is a Wounded Child of Mother Earth

We regret the numerous acts of violence that the land of Australia has experienced at the hands of European settlers and we seek means of regeneration and restoration of the land previously preserved her Aboriginal custodians.

Principle 4 focuses on the suffering experienced by the land of Australia—a child of Mother Earth—at the hands of invading settlers and current inhabitants. The time has come to recognise publicly these acts of violence and find ways both locally and nationally to rejuvenate and restore the damages inflicted on this child of Mother Earth.

The Challenge

This principle challenges us to recognise that:

- we have wounded Mother Earth in many ways
- we need to identify the extent and depth of these wounds
- we ought to search for new ways to heal the wounds.

This principle also challenges us to relate to the land of Australia:

- as a child of Mother Earth who has been badly wounded
- as a child on whom we have inflicted suffering
- as a child whose serious wounds we need to heal.

The Voice of Science

The wounds of our Mother, Planet Earth, are numerous. The exploitation of her forests in many countries is tragic. The pollution of her oceans like the Pacific is painful to behold. Once fertile soils are now saline. Many species—all diverse children of Planet Earth—have become extinct; others are under threat. The magnificent Barrier Reef off the eastern coast of Australia is severely diminished.

The pollution of the Pacific by masses of plastic involves more than an accumulation of plastic waste. The plastic gradually decomposes and micro fragments of plastic are imbibed by fish and other sea creatures. We, in turn, consume these plastic micro fragments when we eat sea creatures.

Especially painful is the way that global warming is now creating wounds that may never heal. Ice scientists, for example, can now measure the decrease in the ice at both the North and South poles. Ice thickness is now half what it was in 1980. The Antarctic is warming twice as fast as other parts of Planet Earth and now affects the seas surrounding the land of Australia. Longer summers make life difficult for creatures of the Arctic such as polar bears. The wounded daughter of Mother Earth is crying out for an end global warming.

The task of healing the land of Australia is not easy. Scientists can identify the wounds, consequences of the ways that humans have treated our land as if she were but lifeless matter. Soil degradation, habitat destruction, erosion and salinity are evident across the globe.

The difficulty is that most nations, including Australia, are bent on economic progress, unlimited growth and exploitation of Planet

Earth. Healing the wounds of the land of Australia requires a complete change of heart and economic policy, and involves a readiness to cease abusing nature and to relate to our land as a wounded daughter of Mother Earth, rather than product to be exploited. The resources of Planet Earth are limited and the current over-use of these resources means that life on this planet may be confined within restricted limits, perhaps no longer viable for many species. Our sacred sanctuary may be violated and desecrated.

There has been some effort to confront the cause and effects of climate change, but most leaders are unwilling to face the fact that global warming is a serious environmental crisis that requires bold action, not token promises. Economic forces tend to control the decision-making processes, even in the land of Australia.

The Voice of the Christian Scriptures

Psalmists often hear the habitats and creatures of Planet Earth praising God and they invite us to join them (for example Ps 148). Many of the prophets, however, also hear Planet Earth crying, mourning and weeping because of her pain. Jeremiah not only experiences pain when he feels the anguish of Planet Earth (Jer 4:19–28); he also observes that God hears the cry of habitats on Planet Earth when these parts of God's vineyard has become a wilderness (Jer 12:10–11). Joel even hears the wild beasts crying out to God because their pastures have been consumed (Joel 1:19–20).

In this context, a second look at Psalm 23:1–4 is illuminating.

The Lord is my shepherd, I shall not want.
He makes me lie down in green pastures,
He leads me beside still waters,
He restores my life.

The Good Shepherd does not restore nature or people with a snap of his fingers: he links healing with nature and leads the sufferer through green pastures, beside still waters. The natural world is where the empathetic shepherd works healing. Why? Because the compassion of the Creator Spirit fills Planet Earth (Ps 33:5).

In Romans 8 we discover an amazing insight from St Paul: the groaning of the Spirit accompanying the groaning of creation is a groaning that anticipates a day of restoration and rebirth (Rom

8:19–27). The Creator Spirit alive within creation is groaning on our behalf—and on behalf of our wounded Mother (Rom 8:26–27).

According to St Paul, in Colossians, the cosmic Christ, is the compassionate presence of the Creator Spirit in creation effecting healing and reconciliation of 'all things', that is, all creation. This reconciliation is linked directly with the suffering of God on the cross to effect 'peace' throughout creation (Col 1:15–20). The God of creation is not only present 'in, with and under' the entire cosmos; the same God also suffers 'in, with and under' all creation—including the land of Australia.

The impulse to show compassion for Planet Earth, therefore, is grounded in more than the call of Planet Earth to be healed. For Christians who affirm the story of the crucifixion, that call is also grounded in the Gospel: the message that the suffering God of the cross is a partner in the task of healing Planet Earth. The call to restore our Mother is a call from the divine depths of creation.

The Voice of the Aboriginal Custodians of Australia

The Aboriginal Peoples of this land can also testify that they have heard the land of Australia crying in pain because of her wounds. The trashing of Maralinga with atomic explosions is one of the many wounds in our land. This is the cry of the Rainbow Spirit elders in *Rainbow Spirit Theology*.

> *The Creator Spirit, also known as the Rainbow Spirit, is crying because the blood of the Aboriginal people has desecrated the land. The land is crying out because the blood on the ground has not been heard, and the sacrifice of those who died has not been remembered* (2007, 48).

> *The Creator Spirit is crying because the deep spiritual bonds with the land and its people have been broken. The land is crying because it is slowly dying without the bond of spiritual life. The people are crying because they long for a restoration of that deep spiritual bond with the Creator Spirit and the land* (2007, 42).

The cries of the land of Australia have also reached the heart and soul of sensitive women surrounded by apparently heartless mining companies. As we listen, we may well hear the cry of one such Aboriginal woman, Mary Duroux.

> *My mother, my mother, what have they done?*
> *Crucified you like the Only Son!*
> *Murder committed by mortal hand.*
> *I weep for my mother, my mother, the land* (1992, 20).

The suffering of the land, according to Galarrwuy Yunupingu, is communicated to those who are sensitive to the language of the land and can read the landscape.

> *I understand that Mother Earth is suffering because there is so much devastation. Trees are dying and have to be cleared away. Lands are being cut by floodwaters, and many types of environmental destruction are taking place. That is when you experience the suffering of the Spirit of the Land, because of the carelessness of the non-Aboriginal people who call themselves 'owners' of this country* (1996, 9–10).

The suffering of the land of Australia experienced by the Aboriginal Peoples is not only a spiritual and cultural reality known to the original custodians of this land; it is also a signal to the settlers of this country and their descendants that the suffering of this land is a profound reality that should be recognised and, with compassion, be healed as part of an ongoing peace process.

The Voice of Planet Earth

I am Earth.
My daughter, the land of Australia,
has experienced the pain and injustice
of brutal injuries
caused by social and political forces
that have treated my daughter
as lifeless matter,
that could be abused
by mining magnates,
nuclear trials
and violent land rapists.

Planet Earth Peace Mission

A peace mission to heal the wounds of the land of Australia is not easy to implement given the forceful economic worldview of our government and much of our society. One of our first tasks is to expose the wounds visually and emotionally through the media and throughout the community. We need not only to see that violence that has been inflicted; we also to feel the pain experienced by the daughter of Mother Earth.

A given community may wish to function like a medico and identify the wounds of the land of Australia in a known location.

In each case the diagnosis would involve determining the cause of the local wounds of Planet Earth; the severity of the wound; past efforts, if any, to heal the wound; ways of exposing the severity of the wound to the wider community, including religious, social and political leaders. In short, we need committed peace advocates to become 'disaster doctors' or 'Planet Earth medics' who are willing not only to identify the nature of the wounds of the land of Australia, but also to publicise our findings regardless of the consequences.

In the Christian context, the religious leaders need not only cite the compassion of Christ for personal healing but also demonstrate how this wounding of Planet Earth moves them to fund ways of healing the land and its diverse inhabitants—including the people of Australia who have been wounded.

Reflections

In response to the voice of Planet Earth here in the land of Australia I have, over the years, reflected personally about my identity as a Planet Earth being and the pains my mother, Planet Earth, has experienced in this land. I include one of these reflections to stimulate further reflection about ways of creating peace with Planet Earth.

The Call of Country

When we arrive at the dry reaches
of Maralinga,
a desolate, desecrated and forsaken site,
where darkness once covered the land
with a thick black cloud of death,

we cross the broken fence that warns
of radioactive fallout still alive
long after the atomic blasts of the 1950s.

We meet a few Aboriginal people
returning to the fringes of the bomb sites
on what was once sacred soil and ask,
'Why are you returning to country?'
'Why?
Because our country is calling us,
crying to be healed.'

We ask them whether their suffering,
from the fallout, the forced removals,
and the wound of their lands,
was worth the sacrifice.
After all, the politicians said,
'We need this land to test these bombs
and keep the world free.'

And they reply,
'They crucified this land
and she is not free.
She is crying deep within,
hoping for a chance to live again.'

Now I too hear the land,
the crucified daughter of Mother Earth,
calling us to heal her wounds.
(Habel 1999, 180)

Chapter Five
Principle 5: Australia Is a Land with a Voice

We ask that the voices of the land of Australia and her Aboriginal custodians be heard so that the government of this land becomes acutely aware not only of the environmental crisis but also of the inalienable rights of the land of Australia and her original custodians.

Principle Five links our concern with that of the Aboriginal Peoples outlined in *The Uluru Statement of the Heart*, a document that calls for all the people of the land of Australia to listen to the voice of the Aboriginal Peoples and incorporate that voice in the constitution of Australia. This principle also asks that the voice and rights of the land of Australia receive comparable recognition as we seek peace with the land.

The Challenge

This principle challenges us to recognise that the land of Australia:

- is a community of habitats and diverse inhabitants of Planet Earth whose voices all need to be heard
- has integral inalienable rights as a discrete continent of Planet Earth
- ought to be treated as a subject, as a child of Planet Earth, rather than as an object.

This principle also challenges us to acknowledge the Aboriginal Peoples

- as having vital and inalienable spiritual custodial rights in the land of Australia
- as peoples whose voice should be heard in our constitution
- as the traditional custodians still awaiting a treaty.

The Voice of Science

Ecology has now revealed that not only are all eco-systems interrelated, but that the elements, entities and beings of these systems communicate as a living web of life. Thomas Berry claims that Planet Earth is also a 'community' in which each being and part of each habitat has a voice.

> *In reality there is a single community of the Earth that includes all its component members, whether human or other than human. In this community every being has its own role to fulfil, its own dignity, its inner spontaneity. Every being has its own voice. Every being declares itself to the entire universe. Every being enters into community with other beings* (Berry 1999, p. 4).

These voices of the 'other than human' components of every biome in the land of Australia is a mystery few seem to hear. Birds' voices may be heard in the forest, but the voices of the forest are rarely the focus of attention. Animal voices may be heard but the voices of the fields are ignored. Rarely do human beings give these voices credibility as sources of wisdom about life and wellbeing in the habitats and communities we share.

We need to listen to the voices of Planet Earth's community of diverse 'component members whether human or other than human'

(Berry 1999, 4)—whether they are songs of celebration or cries of anguish. The diverse voices of the land of Australia are a mystery of Planet Earth we are called to articulate throughout our communities. We need to be prophets for our land and for our kin in the land.

Hearing the voice of Planet Earth is linked to the task of reading the pages of Planet Earth: the bold print of the planet's history, geology and geography as well as the blueprints embedded in designs innate in the planet—especially in the land of Australia.

The understandings of various sciences are vital for us to understand where we belong in the history of the cosmos, what is happening to Planet Earth, and what we need to do to sustain our planet into the future. We need to read the information and hear the messages that are recorded in the landscapes, the volcanoes, the ice caps, the oceans, the deserts, the tectonic plates, the weather—and in every part of the complex community of biomes in this land, whether large or small.

We need scientists who can interpret the pages of this book called Planet Earth and hear the voice of Mother Earth latent in that book. And we need custodians who know how to use the findings of the scientists to sustain the planet.

Vital information is also found in the designs or blueprints located in the depths of life and matter, everything from the DNA in our living cells to the structure of organisms and atoms. Here again we need the tools and skills of modern science to understand the language and message of these blueprints of nature.

The voice of every being or every aspect of the diverse biomes of the land of Australia can readily be affirmed as a mystery of nature, an expression of the identity of that reality. Inherent in the nuances of the concept of 'voice' is a recognition of the rights of that entity; a voice is an expression of its right to exist, and an expression of its character and its right as a member of the Planet Earth community to be free from domination.

If we dare to consider establishing peace with the land of Australia and its diverse human and other than human communities, biomes and habitats, we may well ask whether we have considered the rights of these entities.

> Have we considered not only the flow of the mighty Murray
> but also the river's right to flow freely, to remain unpolluted

> and to sustain the diversity of life in living in and dependent on the river's waters?
>
> Have we recognised not only the beauty of the rainforests but also their right to exist as vibrant expressions of life in the land of Australia?
>
> Have we acknowledged not only the wonders of our amazing landscapes but also their voices expressing their right to be heard communicating their message about how to sustain their future?

The Voice of the Christian Scriptures

The biblical traditions tend to focus on the rights of peoples to possess and own the land. The ideology of the Book of Joshua promotes the status, rights and responsibilities of ancestral households and their heads over the portions of the 'promised land' they believe YHWH, their god, allocated to them. The idea undergirding the Jubilee year demonstrated their belief in the perpetuity of their ownership of their allocated land.

In the proposed rural economy in the text of Leviticus 25–27, however, urban elite landholders—who controlled peasant lands throughout much of Israel's history—are explicitly excluded from authority over, or rights to, the properties of established peasant farmers.

More significant, however, is the tradition that holds YHWH as the divine landowner who demands recognition of the rights of his land, especially in the Sabbath year. On the Sabbath year, the land returns to its owner, to YHWH. The tenants have no rights in that year. Leviticus 25 demonstrates that the divine landowner requires that all cultivation be suspended every seven years; in this year of Sabbath rest, the rights of the land and the divine landowner prevail over those of the human tenants. In that year the land enjoys complete rest from the turmoil of tenants at work (Habel 1995, chapter 6). Whether or not this ideal was ever realised, it is clear that a belief that the land had a right to rest and be restored existed.

Another tradition in the ancient Near East was the treaty procedure, according to which two human bodies—whether nations, communities or individuals—would swear before their god and a witness. Significantly that witness was often a phenomenon of nature, including the land. When the Israelites had broken their treaty/ covenant with their God, Micah calls on these other than human witnesses.

> *Hear, you mountains, the controversy of the Lord,*
> *and you enduring foundations of the land.*
> *For YHWH has a controversy with his people,*
> *and he will contend with Israel* (Micah 6:2).

In the Abraham narratives, Abraham respects the rights of the Canaanites to possess and preserve their land. On one occasion, Abraham makes a treaty with Abimelech and swears before the Canaanite Creator Spirit, El Olam. Abraham not only swears to be loyal to his Canaanite ally, but also to the land where he is sojourning (Gen 21:22–24). The land is recognised as a partner in the treaty.

The Voice of the Aboriginal Custodians of Australia

For millennia the Aboriginal Peoples of the land of Australia have been reading the landscape, discerning the laws of nature and hearing the voices of the spiritual realities in the land. But their capacity to hear and read the landscape has been dismissed. They also hear the voices of the land suffering. As Yunupingu writes, even

> *when I am not on my tribal land I am able to speak sign language. I do the same by looking at hills with no trees. I understand that those hills are suffering. I understand that Mother Earth is suffering because there is so much suffering* (1996, 9–10).

Or as the Rainbow Spirit elders assert, the

> *Creator Spirit is crying because the blood of the Aboriginal Peoples has desecrated the land. The land is crying out because the blood on the ground has not been heard, and the sacrifice of those who died has not been remembered* (1997, 48).

It is one thing to recognise that our Aboriginal custodians can read the landscape and recognise its right to be heard. It is quite another to realise that the reciprocal custodial rights and voices of the Aboriginal

Peoples themselves have still not been fully acknowledged—as the *Uluru Statement of the Heart* makes very clear.

The rights of the land among Aboriginal Peoples is understood to be the Law that is part of the land itself. Deborah Bird Rose quotes the words of Doug Campbell.

> *You see that hill over there. Blackfellow Law like that hill. It never changes. Whitefellow law goes this way and that, all the time changing. Blackfellow Law different. It never changes. Blackfellow Law hard, like a stone, like that hill. The Law is in the ground* (Rose 1992, 56).

That Law is not only eternal and unchanging; it is also understood to create peace, harmony and true justice in society and the land of Australia. The Law of the land is basis for the rights of the land to be maintained among Aboriginal Peoples as traditional custodians, and, I would argue, between the land of Australia and its current inhabitants.

The Voice of Planet Earth

I am Earth.
If you have the capacity
to read the landscape
and hear the voice of the land,
you may well appreciate
that the land of Australia
has not only a voice to be heard
as a living land in crisis,
but also an inalienable right
to be publicly recognised
by all who have been sustained
by her compassionate care.

Planet Earth Peace Mission

Just as there is now a strong move among various organisations to have the Australian government acknowledge the inalienable custodial rights and voices of the Aboriginal Peoples of the land of Australia, we believe that a similar movement ought to be initiated to acknowledge the inalienable rights and voice of the land of Australia itself. Such a movement would be vital in in the promotion of peace with the land that is our home, the source of our being as Planet Earth beings and the locus of our future on Planet Earth.

If we are to seek peace with Planet Earth and its human and other than human communities, biomes and habitats, we need to recognise them as subjects with rights rather than objects to be exploited. We need to relate to the diverse other than human communities, biomes and habitats of the land of Australia—whether it be the mighty Murray or the earthworms and soil in our gardens—as entities that deserve to be treated as valuable partners in the eco-community of Planet Earth where we live.

Reflections

In response to the voice of Planet Earth here in the land of Australia I have, over the years, reflected personally about my identity as a Planet Earth being. I include one of these reflections to stimulate further reflection about ways of creating peace with Earth.

Presence

I sit in a crevice of nature,
a cove on Kangaroo Island.
It is 3 October 2009.

All is still, shimmering still.
No wind or wave stirs the stillness,
yet there is a feeling of presence: intense, close.

It is as if nature has suspended all drives,
all movement,
so that I might feel her primal pulse.
I too am suspended—framed in stillness,
captured in presence.

Soft sounds hover in the stillness.
A lamb bleats in the distance.
The voice of a fisherman rolls in from out to sea.
A soft voice in the stillness—hovering, suspended!
Then silence in the stillness.

Is this the moment Elijah knew
in the cave on God's mountain?

In that cave, according to the storyteller,
God is not in the storm,
not in the earthquake,
not in the bushfire,
but is a silent voice in the stillness.

Upon reflection I realise
that my innate spirit
is sensitive to Presence:
the deep voice of Planet Earth,
the innate Wisdom in Planet Earth
and
the Spirit of the land of Australia
whispering
in the stillness.

Chapter Six
Principle 6: The Land of Australia Has a Sacred Site at Its Centre

The land of Australia is connected by many sacred sites; Uluru is an especially significant sacred site. Uluru could be viewed as a common spiritual symbol of peace for all Australians, regardless of their faith or orientation. All Australians could use Uluru as a spiritual symbol to express peace between themselves and Planet Earth.

The Challenge

This principle challenges us to recognise that the land of Australia,

- has a sacred site recognised by Aboriginal Peoples, the traditional custodians of the land
- has a sacred site that could be recognised by peoples of diverse faiths and perspectives
- has a sacred site that could become the symbol of peace with the land of Australia and with Planet Earth.

The Voice of Science

According to geologists, the origins of Uluru date back around 400 million years to the time that the land of Australia itself is emerging from the oceans. The waters covering the land of Australia recede and evaporate, revealing the under-water formation known as Uluru by the Aboriginal custodians of Australia.

The underwater formation of Uluru was the result of a long period of mountain building and erosion. During this period, the centre of Australia was turned into an inland sea where deposition began in what is now known as the Amadeus Basin. In that basin, limestone, sand and mud were deposited and buried deep below that inland sea.

About 400 million years ago this deposit was subjected to so much pressure it changed from sediment into rock. After a long period of erosion, the hardened welded-together rock of Uluru emerged from the softer rocks. The surface of this monolith has been etched and polished over tens of millions of years to become the majestic Uluru we can now revere.

Uluru, often identified as The Rock (and as Ayers Rock), is an amazing geological phenomenon; at the centre of the land of Australia, Uluru readily evokes a response of awe and wonder. Uluru is a magnificent golden monolith that emerges from the vast flat landscape of the outback—the Red Centre of Australia; Uluru is truly a sacred landmark of the land of Australia.

The Voice of the Aboriginal Custodians of Australia

The Aboriginal Peoples of the land of Australia have a deep consciousness of the spiritual dimensions of the monolith, a place that houses not only the spirits of their ancestors but is also a pivotal point in the landscape of country from which the Creator Spirit emanates to sustain the life lines of the land of Australia. Uluru is indeed a sacred site that visitors would do well not to climb or conquer like Everest, but to embrace with wonder and reverence.

The 'Creator Spirit' is a term to identify the spiritual force that people of many faiths discern in creation—whether in outer space or the land of Australia. According to the Rainbow Spirit elders, the

> *Creator Spirit is known to Aboriginal Australians by many names, including Yiirmbal, Biame, Rainbow Spirit, Paayamu, Biiral, Wandjina and, in Christian times, Father God* (2007, 31).

According to the Rainbow Spirit elders, the Rainbow Spirit has been present deep within the land from the beginning. The Rainbow Spirit is the Creator Spirit who fills the land with numerous life-forces and spiritual forces. Human beings were also created from the land by the Creator Spirit and have the responsibility to cooperate with the Creator Spirit to both care for and to activate the life-forces within the land. These spiritual forces are concentrated at sacred sites, including Uluru. The Creator Spirit is believed to be the true owner of the land of Australia and its waters (Rainbow Spirit Elders 2007, chapter 3).

The Voice of the Christian Scriptures

The Creator Spirit is discerned by believers in numerous faiths. And in many faith traditions the Creator Spirit is a force or presence that not only permeates the land, but is also experienced at sacred sites.

In the Wisdom school of the ancient Near East, the Creator Spirit employs Wisdom as the blueprint in creating the cosmos. Wisdom is a force innate in creation, an expression of the permeating presence of the Creator Spirit (Habel, 2015).

In Colossians, the writer identifies the Christ (Christos) with the Spirit that creates, permeates and reconciles all creation.

> *For in him all things were created, in heaven and on Earth, visible and invisible... He is before all things and in him all things hold together... For in him all the fullness of God was pleased to dwell, and through him to reconcile to himself all things, whether on Earth or in heaven,* ***making peace*** *by the blood of his cross* (Col 1:15–20).

For Christians, the claim that Christos, as the Creator Spirit, is before all things, in all things, unites all things and makes peace with all things is a spiritual consciousness that is not only parallel with that of the Rainbow Spirit elders, but also relevant for an appreciation of the presence of the Creator Spirit in the land of Australia and in Uluru. This Presence effects reconciliation and peace with our Planet Earth as part of the universe.

Symbol of Peace with Planet Earth

If people of faith and other perspectives can view Uluru with a consciousness of deep wonder and also appreciate the presence of a Creator Spirit consciousness or its secular counterpart, then Uluru may well have the potential for being a symbol of peace for all peoples in the land of Australia.

If we watch Uluru at sunset, with each stage of the sunset, the monolith in the heart of Australia changes colour from gold to orange to burning red to purple. The sun seems to be setting inside Uluru revealing a Presence emanating from within the monolith.

Some years ago, when I visited Uluru, I wrote a poem that, I believe, is relevant today.

Uluru

I stood on a hill at sunset
overlooking a massive rock;
a mile high, some say,
and twenty miles around.

The rock was Uluru,
a golden boulder rising from deep in the red centre
of the land of Australia,
a sacred site of Aboriginal Peoples.

As I watched,
wonder surged up within me
as the rock changed colour from instant to instant,
from celestial gold to earthy orange,
from vivid bronze to blazing red to sacred purple—
all the colours of the desert rainbow.

I sensed what many had sensed
in other lands before me,
the point of spiritual concentration,
the navel of Planet Earth
where spirit is incarnate in the rock,
the intrinsic worth of Earth is revealed
and discerning presence
means peace with country.

I sensed too
that my innate spirit had stirred
wonder within me
to connect me spiritually
with an ancient sacred site
in the land of Australia.

If we dare to recognise that Uluru is equivalent to the 'navel of Planet Earth', and a site that reveals the 'worth of Planet Earth'—a sacred place in the sanctuary that is Planet Earth—it is possible to take the next step and recognise the monolith as a vital symbol of peace with Planet Earth and especially with the land of Australia in the current tumultuous environmental context.

The Voice of Planet Earth

I am Earth.
Across my vibrant face
there are many sacred sites
where people of many faiths
have experienced spiritual impulses
emerging from within me.

Uluru is one such site,
a symbol of a much needed treaty
between the peoples of the land of Australia
and a symbol of much needed peace
with me, your compassionate Mother Earth.

Planet Earth Peace Mission

The words of George Rosendale, my Aboriginal mentor, encapsulates the mystery of his spiritual connection with the Creator Spirit and the land of his birth.

> *I am spiritual. Inside me is spirit and land, both given to me by the Creator Spirit. There is a piece of land in me, and it keeps drawing me back like a magnet to the land from which I came. Because the land too is spiritual* (Rainbow Spirit Elders 2007, 12).

If we dare to recognise Uluru as a spiritual symbol—a central sacred site of the land of Australia—we may well sense that we too are being drawn back to by this magnet at the centre of the land to promote peace not only with the Aboriginal Peoples, the custodians of the land, but also with the land itself: the spiritual and biological source of our being as Planet Earth beings and land beings.

The task remains: how do we stir the consciousness of Australians to move beyond viewing the land of Australia as territory to create wealth and Uluru as a famous tourist attraction? How do we generate a deep awareness that Uluru is a magnet drawing us to make peace with the land, with the peoples of the land and with Mother Earth, and with the sacred Presence in the sanctuary land of Australia?

Reflections

In response to the voice of Planet Earth here in the land of Australia I have, over the years, reflected personally about my identity as a Planet Earth being. I include one of these reflections to stimulate further discussion about ways of creating peace with Planet Earth.

Land and Spirit

After more years of searching
the link between land and spirit,
Planet Earth and the spiritual,
nature and my inner self,
I stirred a latent consciousness
that my inner being
was a spiritual self
linked to the land,

this land—
the land of Australia—
as my Aboriginal mentors affirmed.

In each Aboriginal person
there is land and spirit.
Both of these link each one of us
with the land
and the Creator Spirit in the land.
For us Aboriginal Peoples
to know our true identity,
it is vital for us to know
the specific place in the land
where we belong
(Rainbow Spirit Elders 2007, 62).

I believe I can now also say
that within me
there is land and spirit.
I am a Planet Earth being in a land
designed by the Spirit,
permeated by the Spirit,
and a being healed by the Spirit
to create peace.

Appendix A
The Vision of Charles Strong

Ecology and the environmental crisis were not a dominant concern in the world of Charles Strong before 1900 and during the turn the century. Strong, however, was vehemently opposed to any form of violence and a forceful advocate of creating a community at peace.

The vison of Strong was to create a community at peace governed by the universal Spirit. While the vision of Strong focused primarily on the community at peace locally, socially and nationally, there is clear evidence that for Strong peace with nature and Planet Earth is implied. I believe, therefore, that, in the light of our statement on *Making Peace with the Land of Australia*, his famous vision could be reformulated as follows.

1. Jesus interpreted the Kingdom of God to be the Kingdom of cosmic Love, or in popular terms, 'the Way' of the Spirit animating the world to bring peace on and with Planet Earth.

2. The Way is a spiritual path that is free from the demands of doctrine, dated beliefs in the Bible or ecclesiastical control, a Way that makes ecology vital for developing a peace conscious relationship with Planet Earth.
3. Following the Way involves a conscious life of love, social justice and peace between all members of the community both in society and in nature.
4. The goal of living the Way is to enable an active community to become a vehicle of compassion, reconciliation, moral change and, above all, of peace in society and with Planet Earth.
5. Consistent with this goal is the work of the community to counter violence, expose injustice and oppose all forms of environmental destruction.
6. By living the Way an individual can experience the impulse of the Spirit incarnate deep within each of us reaching out for the universal Spirit to create peace at large in nature and society.

To summarise, in the language of Charles Strong, we need to discern Cosmic Love permeating the land of Australia and to cooperate with that Spirit in creating peace on and with Planet Earth.

Bibliography

Balabanski, Vicky. *An Eco-Stoic Reading of Colossians.* (London: Bloomsbury, 2020).

Berry, Thomas. *The Great Work. Our Way into the Future.* (New York: Bell Tower, 1999).

Dodson, Patrick. *The Land Our Mother.* CCIP Occasional Paper No. 9. (Melbourne: Collins Dove, 1973).

Dodson, Michael. 'Land Rights and Social Justice', in Galarrwuy Yunupingu (editor). *Our Land Is Our Life.* (St Lucia: Queensland University Press, 1997), 39–51.

Duroux, Mary. *Dirge for Hidden Art.* (Moruya, NSW: Heritage Publishing, 1992), 20.

Habel, Norman. *The Land Is Mine. Six Biblical Land Ideologies.* (Minneapolis: Fortress Press, 1995).

______. *Reconciliation. Searching for Australia's Soul.* (Preston, Vic.: Mosaic Press, 1999).

______. *Rainbow of Mysteries. Meeting the Sacred in Nature.* (Kelowna, BC: Woodlake, 2012).

______. *Discerning Wisdom in God's Creation.* (Northcote, Vic.: Morning Star, 2015).

______. *The Earth Care Charter and 95 Eco-Theses.* (Adelaide, SA: Lutheran Education Australia, 2017).

Habel, Norman (editor). *Christianity Re-interpreted by Charles Strong.* (Melbourne: Morning Star, 2017).

______. *Remembering Pioneer Australian Pacifist Charles Strong.* (Melbourne: Morning Star, 2018).

Habel, Norman *et al. The Season of Creation. A Preaching Commentary.* (Minneapolis: Fortress, 2011).

Macy, Joanna & John Seed. 'Gaia Meditations', in Robert Gottlieb, (editor) *This Sacred Earth. Religion, Nature, Environment.* (New York: Routledge, 1996).

Mudrooroo. *Us Mob. History, Culture Struggle: An Introduction to Indigenous Australia.* (Sydney: Angus and Robertson, 1995).

Rainbow Spirit Elders. *Rainbow Spirit Theology. Towards an Australian Aboriginal Theology.* (2nd edn; Hindmarsh, SA: ATF Press, 2007).

Rose, D. *Dingo Makes Us Human. Life and Land in an Australian Aboriginal Culture.* (Cambridge: Cambridge University Press, 1992).

Suzuki, David & Amanda McConnell. *The Sacred Balance. Rediscovering Our Place in Nature.* (London: Bantam, 1997).

Suzuki, David & Kathy Vanderlinden. *You Are the Earth.* (Sydney: Allen & Unwin, 1999).

Wainwright, Elaine. 'Peace in the Universe', in *Tui Motu InterIslands*, Issue 237, May 2019, 24–25.

Yunupingu, Galarrwuy. 'Concepts of Land and Spirituality', in Anne Patel Gray (editor) *Aboriginal Spirituality, Present and Future.* (Melbourne: Harper Collins, 1996), 4-10.

Yunupingu, Galarrwuy (editor). *Our Land Is Our Life. Land Rights—Past, Present, Future.* (St Lucia: Queensland University Press, 1997).

CPSIA information can be obtained
at www.ICGtesting.com
Printed in the USA
BVHW021931301219
568172BV00004B/13/P
* 9 7 8 1 9 2 5 6 1 2 9 7 4 *